MW01620344
BLUE
450385119U

TO
FROM
DATE

INSPIRATIONAL

MEMORY BOOK

candacecbure.com | dayspring.com

LUKE 2 (NLT)

The Birth of Jesus

At that time the Roman emperor, Augustus, decreed that a census should be taken throughout the Roman Empire. (This was the first census taken when Quirinius was governor of Syria.) All returned to their own ancestral towns to register for this census. And because Joseph was a descendant of King David, he had to go to Bethlehem in Judea, David's ancient home. He traveled there from the village of Nazareth in Galilee. He took with him Mary, to whom he was engaged, who was now expecting a child.

And while they were there, the time came for her baby to be born. She gave birth to her firstborn son. She wrapped him snugly in strips of cloth and laid him in a manger, because there was no lodging available for them.

The Shepherds and Angels

That night there were shepherds staying in the fields nearby, guarding their flocks of sheep. Suddenly, an angel of the Lord appeared among them, and the radiance of the Lord's glory surrounded them. They were terrified, but the angel reassured them. "Don't be afraid!" he said. "I bring you good news that will bring great joy to all people. The Savior—yes, the Messiah, the Lord—has been born today in Bethlehem, the city of David! And you will recognize him by this sign: You will find a baby wrapped snugly in strips of cloth, lying in a manger."

Suddenly, the angel was joined by a vast host of others—the armies of heaven—praising God and saying, "Glory to God in highest heaven, and peace on earth to those with whom God is pleased."

When the angels had returned to heaven, the shepherds said to each other, "Let's go to Bethlehem! Let's see this thing that has happened, which the Lord has told us about."

They hurried to the village and found Mary and Joseph. And there was the baby, lying in the manger. After seeing him, the shepherds told everyone what had happened and what the angel had said to them about this child. All who heard the shepherds' story were astonished, but Mary kept all these things in her heart and thought about them often. The shepherds went back to their flocks, glorifying and praising God for all they had heard and seen. It was just as the angel had told them.

Jesus Is Presented in the Temple

Eight days later, when the baby was circumcised, he was named Jesus, the name given him by the angel even before he was conceived.

Then it was time for their purification offering, as required by the law of Moses after the birth of a child; so his parents took him to Jerusalem to present him to the Lord. The law of the Lord says, "If a woman's first child is a boy, he must be dedicated to the LORD." So they offered the sacrifice required in the law of the Lord—"either a pair of turtledoves or two young pigeons."

The Prophecy of Simeon

At that time there was a man in Jerusalem named Simeon. He was righteous and devout and was

eagerly waiting for the Messiah to come and rescue Israel. The Holy Spirit was upon him and had revealed to him that he would not die until he had seen the Lord's Messiah. That day the Spirit led him to the Temple. So when Mary and Joseph came to present the baby Jesus to the Lord as the law required, Simeon was there. He took the child in his arms and praised God, saying,

"Sovereign Lord, now let your servant die in peace, as you have promised. I have seen your salvation, which you have prepared for all people. He is a light to reveal God to the nations, and he is the glory of your people Israel!"

Jesus' parents were amazed at what was being said about him. Then Simeon blessed them, and he said to Mary, the baby's mother, "This child is destined to cause many in Israel to fall, and many others to rise. He has been sent as a sign from God, but many will oppose him. As a result, the deepest thoughts of many hearts will be revealed. And a sword will pierce your very soul."

The Prophecy of Anna

Anna, a prophet, was also there in the Temple. She was the daughter of Phanuel from the tribe of Asher, and she was very old. Her husband died when they had been married only seven years. Then she lived as a widow to the age of eighty-four. She never left the Temple but stayed there day and night, worshiping God with fasting and prayer. She came along just as Simeon was talking with Mary and Joseph, and she began praising God. She talked about the child to everyone who had been waiting expectantly for God to rescue Jerusalem.

When Jesus' parents had fulfilled all the requirements of the law of the Lord, they returned home to Nazareth in Galilee. There the child grew up healthy and strong. He was filled with wisdom, and God's favor was on him.

Jesus Speaks with the Teachers

Every year Jesus' parents went to Jerusalem for the Passover festival. When Jesus was twelve years old, they attended the festival as usual. After the celebration was over, they started home to Nazareth, but Jesus stayed behind in Jerusalem. His parents didn't miss him at first, because they assumed he was among the other travelers. But when he didn't show up that evening, they started looking for him among their relatives and friends.

When they couldn't find him, they went back to Jerusalem to search for him there. Three days later they finally discovered him in the Temple, sitting among the religious teachers, listening to them and asking questions. All who heard him were amazed at his understanding and his answers.

His parents didn't know what to think. "Son," his mother said to him, "why have you done this to us? Your father and I have been frantic, searching for you everywhere."

"But why did you need to search?" he asked. "Didn't you know that I must be in my Father's house?" But they didn't understand what he meant. Then he returned to Nazareth with them and was obedient to them. And his mother stored all these things in her heart. Jesus grew in wisdom and in stature and in favor with God and all the people.

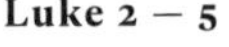

MY FA

HUSBAND

NAME BIRTHPLACE DATES

PARENTS

Father

NAME

BIRTHPLACE DATES

Mother

NAME

BIRTHPLACE DATES

GRANDPARENTS

Paternal

GRANDFATHER

BIRTHPLACE DATES

GRANDMOTHER

BIRTHPLACE DATES

Maternal

GRANDFATHER

BIRTHPLACE DATES

GRANDMOTHER

BIRTHPLACE DATES

GREAT-GRANDPARENTS

Paternal

GRANDFATHER'S FATHER

BIRTHPLACE DATES

GRANDFATHER'S MOTHER

BIRTHPLACE DATES

GRANDMOTHER'S FATHER

BIRTHPLACE DATES

GRANDMOTHER'S MOTHER

BIRTHPLACE DATES

Maternal

GRANDFATHER'S FATHER

BIRTHPLACE DATES

GRANDFATHER'S MOTHER

BIRTHPLACE DATES

GRANDMOTHER'S FATHER

BIRTHPLACE DATES

GRANDMOTHER'S MOTHER

BIRTHPLACE DATES

Y TREE

NAME | BIRTHPLACE | DATES

PARENTS

Father

NAME

BIRTHPLACE | DATES

Mother

NAME

BIRTHPLACE | DATES

GRANDPARENTS

Paternal

GRANDFATHER

BIRTHPLACE | DATES

GRANDMOTHER

BIRTHPLACE | DATES

Maternal

GRANDFATHER

BIRTHPLACE | DATES

GRANDMOTHER

BIRTHPLACE | DATES

GREAT-GRANDPARENTS

Paternal

GRANDFATHER'S FATHER

BIRTHPLACE | DATES

GRANDFATHER'S MOTHER

BIRTHPLACE | DATES

GRANDMOTHER'S FATHER

BIRTHPLACE | DATES

GRANDMOTHER'S MOTHER

BIRTHPLACE | DATES

Maternal

GRANDFATHER'S FATHER

BIRTHPLACE | DATES

GRANDFATHER'S MOTHER

BIRTHPLACE | DATES

GRANDMOTHER'S FATHER

BIRTHPLACE | DATES

GRANDMOTHER'S MOTHER

BIRTHPLACE | DATES

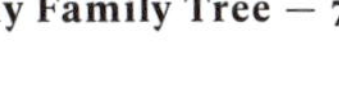

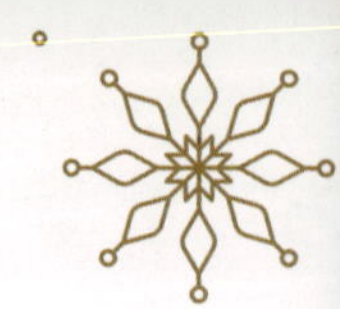

FAVORITE FAMILY CHRISTMAS

CHRISTMAS MEMORIES

INTRODUCTION

Ever since I was a little girl, Christmas has been my favorite time of year. At first it was the sheer joy of all the sights and lights, music in the air, and the promise of exciting things under the tree on Christmas morning! As I grew older, Christmas took on the meaning of family and loved ones close. And finally, when I came to understand the significance of celebrating Jesus, that put an exclamation point on the reason that Christmas held so much delight and anticipation for me. It's all just so *fun*! The chance to dress up in fuzzy sweaters and warm boots, or bright red fancy dresses with furry white trim. Music floating on air as we shop and dream at store windows. And hopefully, our arms wrapped around those who mean the most to us.

When I became a mom, I got to watch the glow on my kids' faces as Christmas invited them into a whole new level of wonder. I'm so thankful for every photo and memory I recorded when Natasha, Lev, and Maks were little. And it has truly been special to be able to capture the moments that my own parents share with my kids each Christmas. Now that they're grown, my kids will be able to look back on the legacy of Camerons and Bures that they came from, sharing traditions and the joy of Jesus' birth with their own families and loved ones for years to come.

The Bible is full of *ebenezers*: memorials set up so that people could look back at all that God had done in their lives. That's what I think of when I journal or take photos. And it's why I wanted to find a way to keep the most significant Christmas memories all in one place. It's my prayer for you as you turn the pages in this journal, to record the best bits of each Christmas, to focus on the uniqueness of your own family celebrations, and to thank God for giving us such special ways to celebrate the coming of the Savior of the world.

XO

Candace

HOW TO USE THIS MEMORY BOOK

You're going to love this! Throughout the following pages, you'll find fun prompts to help you record all your Christmas memories over a five-year period. And when this book is complete, you'll hold in your hands a very meaningful keepsake—one you will enjoy for years to come.

What to Expect

Every year starts with your family Christmas photo and is followed by Candace's Christmas Corner, where you'll find some ideas from me about how to get into the holiday spirit. Then, simply fill in the blanks! You'll record everything from how you decorated your house to your favorite recipe of the season (even the price of eggnog). And when Christmas is over, you'll put it in a safe place and bring it out next year—you'll do this for five years before filling up this book and then possibly starting a brand-new one.

No Rules

One more thing! There are no rules here—this is *your* Christmas Memory Book. You can skip a year (or two) if things get too hectic. You can glue in your photo or you can draw a portrait of your group. You can choose to use the back pocket for Christmas cards or gift tags. You can fill this out during the Christmas season, or you can wait until after the holidays—it is *completely* up to you.

Ready for the most wonderful time of the year? Grab your pen (or your pencil, or your markers, or your washi tape, or your photos—it's your world) and get ready to create one really amazing book that will bring you joy year after year.

WELCOME

OUR PHOTO CARD
OR FAMILY PHOTO

Candace's Christmas Corner

HOLIDAY HOSPITALITY

One of the best ways to get into the holiday spirit is to love one another! That's something we can do all year round, of course. But during the holidays, it just seems like there are more and more opportunities to share our homes and hearts with other people.

Practicing hospitality is actually talked about in the Bible. It's something that believers are supposed to do! But the *heart* of hospitality begins just there: the heart. Being hospitable means treating someone with a welcoming and warm attitude. It might mean letting the frazzled mama who is trying to Christmas shop with two littles in tow cut in front of you at Starbucks. It might mean serving a meal at a local shelter. And yes, it might mean setting a place at the table for someone you normally wouldn't choose to eat with. Hospitality is a choice we make to show others that they belong. And amazingly, most of the time, opening our hearts or homes fills us with a deeper sense of gratitude and purpose as well—even if it might feel uncomfortable at first.

Some of my best memories include kindnesses among strangers. Our Christmas memories, while largely involving close family and friends, are sprinkled with photos and stories of stepping out of our comfort zone to be the light of Jesus to others. If variety is the spice of life, then showing hospitality might just be the spice in that warm cider simmering on the stove in our hearts.

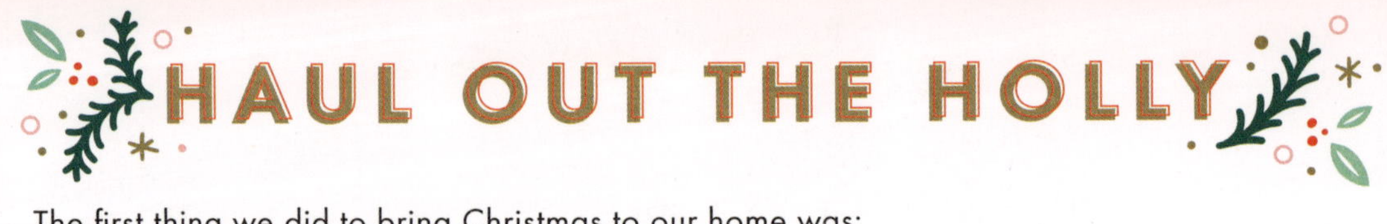

The first thing we did to bring Christmas to our home was:

Date we started playing Christmas music

Date we put up a tree

Date we sent Christmas cards

Date we received our first Christmas card

Date we attended our first party

Here's how we decorated:

SOME OF OUR DECORATIONS

Our December calendar looked like this:

DECEMBER

SUN	MON	TUES	WED	THURS	FRI	SAT

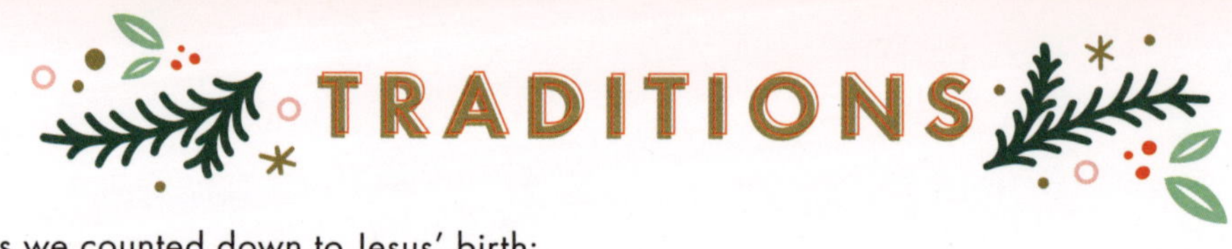

TRADITIONS

Ways we counted down to Jesus' birth:

Our family celebration looked a little like this:

A family recipe we made (and who made it):

Specific ornaments that went on the tree:

Our most special family tradition looked like this:

A new tradition we started (and hope to continue!):

The most memorable event was:

The best light display we saw:

The best movie we watched:

Old favorite movie	New favorite movie

Books that bring the merry:

Old favorite book	New favorite book

This year, we hopped in the car and went . . .

This year, church looked like . . .

THE GIFT THAT KEEPS GIVING

CATEGORY	GIFT	GIVEN BY	GIVEN TO
Favorite			
Funniest			
Most thoughtful			
Most meaningful			
Smallest			
Biggest			
Cutest			
Ugliest			

Important story about one of the gifts:

Story about an act of kindness witnessed or shared:

We are:

- [ ] Team Cutting It Down in the Forest
- [ ] Team Picking It Out at a Tree Lot
- [ ] Team Storing It in the Attic

We have:

- [ ] One big tree for everyone
- [ ] Multiple trees around the house
- [ ] One inside, one outside
- [ ] Other: ______________________________

We have:

- [ ] Coordinated ornaments (by color, shape, size, theme)
- [ ] A mishmash of memories
- [ ] Other: ______________________________

A memory of this year's tree:

PLACE OR DRAW A PICTURE OF YOUR TREE HERE

Songs heard around our house at Christmas:

Musical events near us:

At church, we sang:

Favorite carols:

Least favorite Christmas songs:

A song memory this year:

FOOD, FESTIVE FOOD

The dish that was the star of the show:

Made by

And the recipe is (write it or tape it in below) . . .

TITLE:

PREP TIME: COOK TIME: SERVES:

INGREDIENTS:

DIRECTIONS:

Recipe tips and tricks:

Best cookie of the year: ____________________

Made by ____________________

And the recipe is (write it or tape it in below) . . .

TITLE: ____________________

PREP TIME: __________ COOK TIME: __________ SERVES: __________

INGREDIENTS: ____________________

DIRECTIONS: ____________________

Recipe tips and tricks: ____________________

THE CHRIST IN CHRISTMAS

Our traditions, ideas, and activities that celebrate Jesus:

Our family's biggest prayers this year:

ADVENT SUNDAYS THIS YEAR

Week 1, Hope

DATE

How has Jesus been our hope this year?

Week 2, Peace

DATE

How has Jesus been our peace this year?

Week 3, Joy

DATE

How has Jesus been our joy this year?

Week 4, Love

DATE

How has Jesus been love to us this year?

The little ones this year (ages and stages):

Cute things the kids said:

Favorite moments with littles:

CUTE KIDDOS GO HERE

Prices this year

Eggnog $ ______	Apple cider $ ______
Turkey per lb. $ ______	Our tree $ ______

The weather on Christmas Day

___

___

___

___

___

___

Trending gifts

___

___

___

___

___

___

___

___

Noteworthy headlines

Family news of this year

PASTE THIS
YEAR'S USPS
STAMP HERE

WHAT WE DID ON CHRISTMAS EVE

HOW I WILL REMEMBER CHRISTMAS THIS YEAR

WHAT WE DID ON CHRISTMAS DAY

MY HOPES FOR THE NEW YEAR

WELCOME

OUR PHOTO CARD
OR FAMILY PHOTO
Year

Candace's Christmas Corner

CARDS THAT MATTER

I'll just admit it now: I don't always get my Christmas cards out the door by Christmas. It's a lot of work, to be honest. There's so much pressure to say just the right things, to update family and friends with stories and news of the year. Over the years it's gotten harder for me to keep up with Christmas card etiquette and information.

One of the most freeing things I figured out is that I could reimagine the purpose of my Christmas card sending. At some point, it became less about informing others of the Bure family and more about encouraging the people that enrich our lives. That meant our card sending became more thoughtful, more meaningful, and more fun.

Some people send out hundreds of photo cards, and that's wonderful. But another option is to spend some time thinking about the people you and your family interact with throughout the year. Who has made your life better? A teacher? A gardener? The woman who is always helpful when you have trouble at the grocery self-check, *again*? Who in your life would really benefit from hearing, "Hey, I see you! You've mattered to us. Merry Christmas." You can use the Christmas card opportunity to say words that will truly bless the heart of the person who opens it. And if that's the route you take, then your own card-sending experience will be time very well spent.

The first thing we did to bring Christmas to our home was:

Date we started playing Christmas music

Date we put up a tree

Date we sent Christmas cards

Date we received our first Christmas card

Date we attended our first party

Here's how we decorated:

SOME OF OUR DECORATIONS

Our December calendar looked like this:

DECEMBER

SUN	MON	TUES	WED	THURS	FRI	SAT

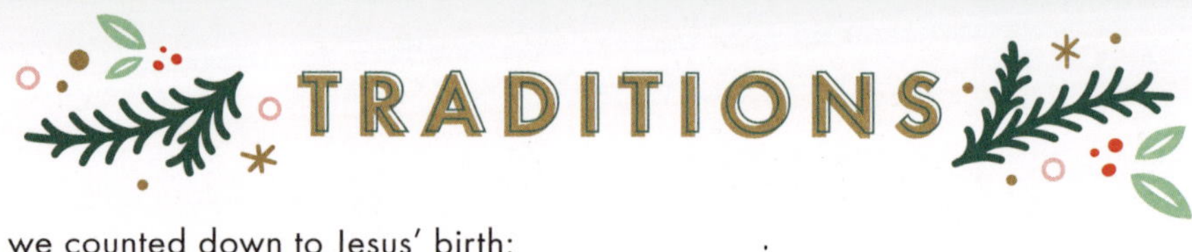

Ways we counted down to Jesus' birth:

Our family celebration looked a little like this:

A family recipe we made (and who made it):

Specific ornaments that went on the tree:

Our most special family tradition looked like this:

A new tradition we started (and hope to continue!):

The most memorable event was:

The best light display we saw:

The best movie we watched:

Old favorite movie	New favorite movie

Books that bring the merry:

Old favorite book	New favorite book

This year, we hopped in the car and went . . .

This year, church looked like . . .

THE GIFT THAT KEEPS GIVING

CATEGORY	GIFT	GIVEN BY	GIVEN TO
Favorite			
Funniest			
Most thoughtful			
Most meaningful			
Smallest			
Biggest			
Cutest			
Ugliest			

Important story about one of the gifts:

Story about an act of kindness witnessed or shared:

We are:

- ☐ Team Cutting It Down in the Forest
- ☐ Team Picking It Out at a Tree Lot
- ☐ Team Storing It in the Attic

We have:

- ☐ One big tree for everyone
- ☐ Multiple trees around the house
- ☐ One inside, one outside
- ☐ Other: ______________________________

We have:

- ☐ Coordinated ornaments (by color, shape, size, theme)
- ☐ A mishmash of memories
- ☐ Other: ______________________________

A memory of this year's tree:

PLACE OR DRAW A PICTURE OF YOUR TREE HERE

Songs heard around our house at Christmas:

Musical events near us:

At church, we sang:

Favorite carols:

Least favorite Christmas songs:

A song memory this year:

The dish that was the star of the show:

Made by

And the recipe is (write it or tape it in below) . . .

TITLE:

PREP TIME: COOK TIME: SERVES:

INGREDIENTS:

DIRECTIONS:

Recipe tips and tricks:

Best cookie of the year: ______________________________

____

____

____

____

____

____

____

Made by ______________________________

And the recipe is (write it or tape it in below) . . .

TITLE: ______________________________

PREP TIME: __________ **COOK TIME:** __________ **SERVES:** __________

INGREDIENTS: ______________________________

____

____

____

____

DIRECTIONS: ______________________________

____

____

____

____

____

Recipe tips and tricks: ______________________________

____

____

THE CHRIST IN CHRISTMAS

Our traditions, ideas, and activities that celebrate Jesus:

Our family's biggest prayers this year:

ADVENT SUNDAYS THIS YEAR

Week 1, Hope

DATE

How has Jesus been our hope this year?

Week 2, Peace

DATE

How has Jesus been our peace this year?

Week 3, Joy

DATE

How has Jesus been our joy this year?

Week 4, Love

DATE

How has Jesus been love to us this year?

The little ones this year (ages and stages):

Cute things the kids said:

Favorite moments with littles:

CUTE KIDDOS GO HERE

Prices this year

Eggnog $________	Apple cider $________
Turkey per lb. $________	Our tree $________

The weather on Christmas Day

Trending gifts

Noteworthy headlines

Family news of this year

PASTE THIS
YEAR'S USPS
STAMP HERE

WHAT WE DID ON CHRISTMAS EVE

HOW I WILL REMEMBER CHRISTMAS THIS YEAR

MY HOPES FOR THE NEW YEAR

WELCOME

OUR PHOTO CARD
OR FAMILY PHOTO

Candace's Christmas Corner

THE GIFTS THAT GIVE

Which do you like better, giving gifts or receiving them? That seems like an obvious answer to some: receiving gifts is great! But I've really come to enjoy the process of giving gifts too.

Giving gifts at Christmas doesn't have to be an expensive project. And I believe it doesn't have to be stressful, either! Here are a few things I do to help me enjoy gift-giving for Christmas:

1. First, pray! This might not seem like an obvious step, but God is the giver of very good gifts. And He knows each person so well. Ask Him how you can bless someone you care about, and He may just share some wonderful gift ideas.

2. Think outside the box. A gift can be an experience, some heartfelt words in a letter, or a meaningful symbol. A friend once surprised me with a fresh orange, and because of an experience we'd had together, I understood exactly why. A piece of fruit brought me to tears!

3. Find a large bin that you can store in the closet. As you find "just right" ideas for someone throughout the year, put them in the bin. By the time December rolls around, you might even be done shopping.

4. Schedule time for wrapping. I like to turn on a classic Christmas movie and use that time to wrap gifts. Gather supplies ahead of time, watch how-to videos online if you need, and add your own touch to the outside of each gift to show how much you care.

5. Be intentional about praying for the person you're giving the gift to. As you wrap it, or as they open it, thank God for how they've blessed you and ask Him to bring them even more blessing in the year to come.

The first thing we did to bring Christmas to our home was:

Date we started playing Christmas music

Date we put up a tree

Date we sent Christmas cards

Date we received our first Christmas card

Date we attended our first party

Here's how we decorated:

SOME OF OUR DECORATIONS

Our December calendar looked like this:

DECEMBER

SUN	MON	TUES	WED	THURS	FRI	SAT

Ways we counted down to Jesus' birth:

Our family celebration looked a little like this:

A family recipe we made (and who made it):

Specific ornaments that went on the tree:

Our most special family tradition looked like this:

A new tradition we started (and hope to continue!):

The most memorable event was:

The best light display we saw:

The best movie we watched:

Old favorite movie	New favorite movie

Books that bring the merry:

Old favorite book	New favorite book

This year, we hopped in the car and went . . .

This year, church looked like . . .

THE GIFT THAT KEEPS GIVING

CATEGORY	GIFT	GIVEN BY	GIVEN TO
Favorite			
Funniest			
Most thoughtful			
Most meaningful			
Smallest			
Biggest			
Cutest			
Ugliest			

Important story about one of the gifts:

Story about an act of kindness witnessed or shared:

O CHRISTMAS TREE!

We are:

- [ ] Team Cutting It Down in the Forest
- [ ] Team Picking It Out at a Tree Lot
- [ ] Team Storing It in the Attic

We have:

- [ ] One big tree for everyone
- [ ] Multiple trees around the house
- [ ] One inside, one outside
- [ ] Other: ____________________

We have:

- [ ] Coordinated ornaments (by color, shape, size, theme)
- [ ] A mishmash of memories
- [ ] Other: ____________________

A memory of this year's tree:

PLACE OR DRAW A PICTURE OF YOUR TREE HERE

Songs heard around our house at Christmas:

Musical events near us:

At church, we sang:

Favorite carols:

Least favorite Christmas songs:

A song memory this year:

The dish that was the star of the show:

Made by

And the recipe is (write it or tape it in below) . . .

TITLE:

PREP TIME: COOK TIME: SERVES:

INGREDIENTS:

DIRECTIONS:

Recipe tips and tricks:

Best cookie of the year:

Made by

And the recipe is (write it or tape it in below) . . .

TITLE:

PREP TIME: **COOK TIME:** **SERVES:**

INGREDIENTS:

DIRECTIONS:

Recipe tips and tricks:

THE CHRIST IN CHRISTMAS

Our traditions, ideas, and activities that celebrate Jesus:

Our family's biggest prayers this year:

ADVENT SUNDAYS THIS YEAR

Week 1, Hope

DATE

How has Jesus been our hope this year?

Week 2, Peace

DATE

How has Jesus been our peace this year?

Week 3, Joy

DATE

How has Jesus been our joy this year?

Week 4, Love

DATE

How has Jesus been love to us this year?

KIDS MAKE CHRISTMAS SPARKLE

The little ones this year (ages and stages):

Cute things the kids said:

Favorite moments with littles:

CUTE KIDDOS GO HERE

Prices this year

Eggnog $______________	Apple cider $______________
Turkey per lb. $______________	Our tree $______________

The weather on Christmas Day

____

____

____

____

____

____

Trending gifts

____

____

____

____

____

____

____

____

Noteworthy headlines

Family news of this year

PASTE THIS
YEAR'S USPS
STAMP HERE

WHAT WE DID ON CHRISTMAS EVE

HOW I WILL REMEMBER CHRISTMAS THIS YEAR

MY HOPES FOR THE NEW YEAR

WELCOME

OUR PHOTO CARD
OR FAMILY PHOTO

Candace's Christmas Corner

RECIPES FOR JOY

My family loves cooking, especially during the holidays. I love the feeling of pulling out the special bakeware and serving dishes that have graced our table for years, or even generations. I love using the slightly flour-stained index cards in my grandmother's handwriting, trying to get that one recipe to taste the way it did when she made it. And I love bringing a new dish to the table too—something that adds variety to our meals and just might become a family tradition down the line!

Food has a special way of bringing us together at Christmastime. Whether it's a batch of red and green cookies, two mugs of steaming cocoa, the special vegetarian dish you make for your friend who's not a turkey fan, or pulling out the potato ricer that only appears during your holiday celebrations, the time we spend in the kitchen is an opportunity to connect with our loved ones. What's on our table, in the end, is less important than who is joining us around it.

Even in the first-century church, breaking bread together was important. The Bible says they got together, prayed, studied Scripture, and ate. There's something very special about sharing a meal. Christmas is such a wonderful time to honor our roots. Put a little extra love into the meals and moments gathered around the table this year. It's sure to make the memories extra sweet.

HAUL OUT THE HOLLY

The first thing we did to bring Christmas to our home was:

Date we started playing Christmas music

Date we put up a tree

Date we sent Christmas cards

Date we received our first Christmas card

Date we attended our first party

Here's how we decorated:

SOME OF OUR DECORATIONS

Our December calendar looked like this:

SUN	MON	TUES	WED	THURS	FRI	SAT

Ways we counted down to Jesus' birth:

Our family celebration looked a little like this:

A family recipe we made (and who made it):

Specific ornaments that went on the tree:

Our most special family tradition looked like this:

A new tradition we started (and hope to continue!):

The most memorable event was:

The best light display we saw:

The best movie we watched:

Old favorite movie	New favorite movie

Books that bring the merry:

Old favorite book	New favorite book

This year, we hopped in the car and went . . .

This year, church looked like . . .

THE GIFT THAT KEEPS GIVING

CATEGORY	GIFT	GIVEN BY	GIVEN TO
Favorite			
Funniest			
Most thoughtful			
Most meaningful			
Smallest			
Biggest			
Cutest			
Ugliest			

Important story about one of the gifts:

Story about an act of kindness witnessed or shared:

We are:

- ☐ Team Cutting It Down in the Forest
- ☐ Team Picking It Out at a Tree Lot
- ☐ Team Storing It in the Attic

We have:

- ☐ One big tree for everyone
- ☐ Multiple trees around the house
- ☐ One inside, one outside
- ☐ Other: ______________________________

We have:

- ☐ Coordinated ornaments (by color, shape, size, theme)
- ☐ A mishmash of memories
- ☐ Other: ______________________________

A memory of this year's tree:

____

____

____

____

____

____

____

____

____

____

PLACE OR DRAW A PICTURE OF YOUR TREE HERE

Songs heard around our house at Christmas:

Musical events near us:

At church, we sang:

Favorite carols:

Least favorite Christmas songs:

A song memory this year:

The dish that was the star of the show:

Made by

And the recipe is (write it or tape it in below) . . .

TITLE:

PREP TIME: COOK TIME: SERVES:

INGREDIENTS:

DIRECTIONS:

Recipe tips and tricks:

Best cookie of the year:

Made by

And the recipe is (write it or tape it in below) . . .

TITLE:

PREP TIME: COOK TIME: SERVES:

INGREDIENTS:

DIRECTIONS:

Recipe tips and tricks:

THE CHRIST IN CHRISTMAS

Our traditions, ideas, and activities that celebrate Jesus:

Our family's biggest prayers this year:

ADVENT SUNDAYS THIS YEAR

Week 1, Hope

DATE

How has Jesus been our hope this year?

Week 2, Peace

DATE

How has Jesus been our peace this year?

Week 3, Joy

DATE

How has Jesus been our joy this year?

Week 4, Love

DATE

How has Jesus been love to us this year?

KIDS MAKE CHRISTMAS SPARKLE

The little ones this year (ages and stages):

Cute things the kids said:

Favorite moments with littles:

CUTE KIDDOS GO HERE

Prices this year

Eggnog $ ______	Apple cider $ ______
Turkey per lb. $ ______	Our tree $ ______

The weather on Christmas Day

______
______
______
______
______
______

Trending gifts

______
______
______
______
______
______
______
______

Noteworthy headlines

Family news of this year

PASTE THIS
YEAR'S USPS
STAMP HERE

HOW I WILL REMEMBER CHRISTMAS THIS YEAR

MY HOPES FOR THE NEW YEAR

WELCOME

OUR PHOTO CARD
OR FAMILY PHOTO

Candace's Christmas Corner

THE CHRIST IN CHRISTMAS

On the first Christmas night, God made sure the whole world knew something was different. He placed a huge, bright star in the sky over the stable where His Son Jesus was born. Angels filled the sky with music and celebration. They made so much racket that shepherds tending their flocks in a field couldn't help but go into town to see the baby Savior for themselves. The story that fascinates me, though, is the wise men from the East. These men were astronomers and experts in their religious field. They saw the unusual star and started traveling. It took them two years to find Jesus, but they somehow sensed the importance of following that star to the end. And when they got there, the Bible says they worshiped Him.

The fact that Jesus came to live among humans, then take our sins upon Himself so that we could be forever united with God, gives us all the hope in the world. A tiny baby, born in a stable in the Middle East two thousand years ago, means that you and I have every reason to celebrate.

There are lots of reasons we keep our faith to ourselves. Lots of reasons we don't trumpet "Jesus is the reason for Christmas!" every time we go out in public. But Jesus is the light that this world needs! Every year, my family and I talk about the best ways we can share Jesus at Christmastime. There are things we always do, and things we do only once or twice. But we intentionally keep Jesus at the center of our hearts and minds. I encourage you to do the same with your family. Go to church and post about it. Wear the shirt that talks about love coming down. Share a Scripture. Serve others. Love well. Don't be shy—shine! And if you do, your holidays will be better for it. That's a promise.

The first thing we did to bring Christmas to our home was:

Date we started playing Christmas music

Date we put up a tree

Date we sent Christmas cards

Date we received our first Christmas card

Date we attended our first party

Here's how we decorated:

SOME OF OUR DECORATIONS

Our December calendar looked like this:

DECEMBER

SUN	MON	TUES	WED	THURS	FRI	SAT

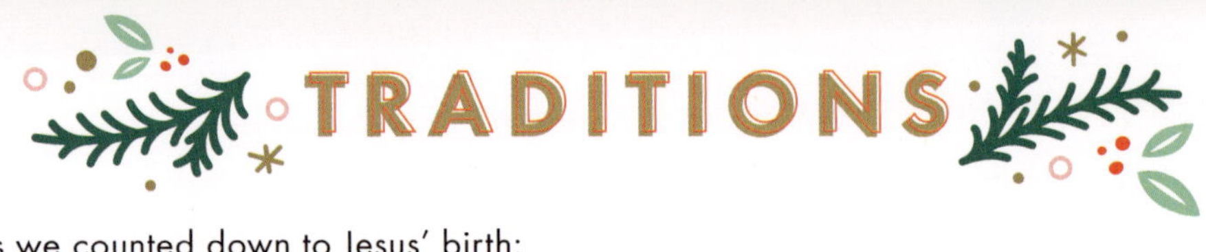

Ways we counted down to Jesus' birth:

Our family celebration looked a little like this:

A family recipe we made (and who made it):

Specific ornaments that went on the tree:

Our most special family tradition looked like this:

A new tradition we started (and hope to continue!):

PLACES & EVENTS

The most memorable event was:

The best light display we saw:

The best movie we watched:

Old favorite movie	New favorite movie

Books that bring the merry:

Old favorite book	New favorite book

This year, we hopped in the car and went . . .

This year, church looked like . . .

THE GIFT THAT KEEPS GIVING

CATEGORY	GIFT	GIVEN BY	GIVEN TO
Favorite			
Funniest			
Most thoughtful			
Most meaningful			
Smallest			
Biggest			
Cutest			
Ugliest			

Important story about one of the gifts:

Story about an act of kindness witnessed or shared:

O CHRISTMAS TREE!

We are:

- [ ] Team Cutting It Down in the Forest
- [ ] Team Picking It Out at a Tree Lot
- [ ] Team Storing It in the Attic

We have:

- [ ] One big tree for everyone
- [ ] Multiple trees around the house
- [ ] One inside, one outside
- [ ] Other: ______________________

We have:

- [ ] Coordinated ornaments (by color, shape, size, theme)
- [ ] A mishmash of memories
- [ ] Other: ______________________

A memory of this year's tree:

PLACE OR DRAW A PICTURE OF YOUR TREE HERE

Songs heard around our house at Christmas:

Musical events near us:

At church, we sang:

Favorite carols:

Least favorite Christmas songs:

A song memory this year:

The dish that was the star of the show:

Made by

And the recipe is (write it or tape it in below) . . .

TITLE:

PREP TIME: COOK TIME: SERVES:

INGREDIENTS:

DIRECTIONS:

Recipe tips and tricks:

Best cookie of the year:

Made by

And the recipe is (write it or tape it in below) . . .

TITLE:

PREP TIME: COOK TIME: SERVES:

INGREDIENTS:

DIRECTIONS:

Recipe tips and tricks:

THE CHRIST IN CHRISTMAS

Our traditions, ideas, and activities that celebrate Jesus:

Our family's biggest prayers this year:

ADVENT SUNDAYS THIS YEAR

Week 1, Hope

DATE

How has Jesus been our hope this year?

Week 2, Peace

DATE

How has Jesus been our peace this year?

Week 3, Joy

DATE

How has Jesus been our joy this year?

Week 4, Love

DATE

How has Jesus been love to us this year?

KIDS MAKE CHRISTMAS SPARKLE

The little ones this year (ages and stages):

Cute things the kids said:

Favorite moments with littles:

CUTE KIDDOS GO HERE

Prices this year

Eggnog $ ________	Apple cider $ ________
Turkey per lb. $ ________	Our tree $ ________

The weather on Christmas Day

____
____
____
____
____
____

Trending gifts

____
____
____
____
____
____
____
____

Noteworthy headlines

Family news of this year

PASTE THIS
YEAR'S USPS
STAMP HERE

HOW I WILL REMEMBER CHRISTMAS THIS YEAR

WHAT WE DID ON CHRISTMAS DAY

MY HOPES FOR THE NEW YEAR

Want more from Candace?

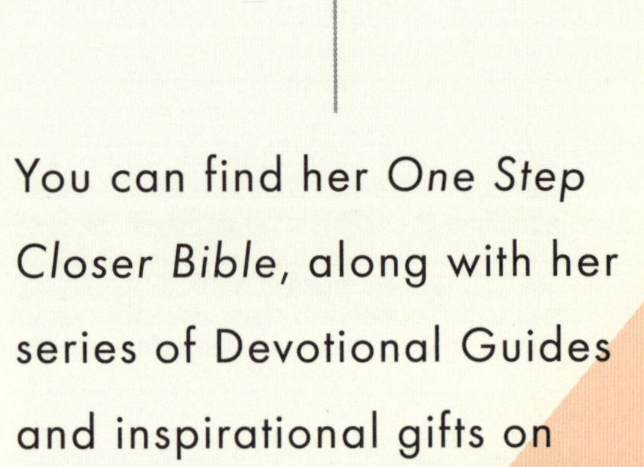

You can find her *One Step Closer Bible*, along with her series of Devotional Guides and inspirational gifts on *dayspring.com*, as well as several retail stores near you.

About the Author

CANDACE CAMERON BURE is an actress, producer, and *New York Times* bestselling author. She is beloved by millions worldwide for her roles as DJ Tanner in the iconic family sitcoms *Full House* and *Fuller House*, in Hallmark Channel movies, as former cohost of *The View*, and as a *Dancing with the Stars* season 18 finalist. Candace is both outspoken and passionate about her family and faith. She and her husband, Val, have been married for 25 years. They have three grown children and live with their much-loved dog, Boris, in the LA area.

First Edition, May 2022

Published by:

21154 Highway 16 East
Siloam Springs, AR 72761
dayspring.com

Additional content collaboration provided by: Trieste Vaillancourt
Cover Design by: Jessica Wei

Printed in China
Prime: J8531
ISBN: 978-1-64870-798-8